This book was written by: Teresa Connor

Illustrations drawn by: Holly Thrailkill

We are both victims and survivors of childhood sexual abuse.

I want to thank Holly for her help and inspiration, without whom these

drawings would never have been completed. She is a very naturally talented

artist. I would also like to thank her for her friendship & support.

Dear Parents/Grandparents,

This book was written to guide you in talking to your child/children about inappropriate touching or sexual abuse. I know it is a very difficult thing to discuss especially with a child. But it is something I feel strongly about and don't feel we educate our children enough on this terrible subject. We need to educate them so they can learn the signs and protect themselves. I was sexually abused as a child by an uncle who I trusted. He told me not to tell, that no one would believe me. Because I didn't tell, the abuse continued for several years. I even blocked most of it out of my memory until just recently. Due to this I grew up ashamed, feeling dirty, unloved, invisible, and not worthy of love and affection.

Because I grew up this way, I talked to my children about this difficult subject and intend to continue with my grandchildren. My daughter has already started talking to her two daughters, the oldest is nine and has already read this book.

I felt led to write this to help others have a tool to aid them in talking to their children and educate them for their protection. And hopefully keep them safe from this horrible crime against children. I hope and pray this book will help you as you open the subject to where your child will feel they can talk to you.

There is nothing explicit in this book. I've left it very open for each family to carry the discussion further if you feel you child is old enough or has questions. I recommend you read it through first to prepare for possible questions your child may have. Also if your child shows no signs of upset and seems to understand you may want to stop on page nine or ten, depending on how young your child is. But if your child shows changes in behavior, gets upset or doesn't want to continue reading, then there may be a problem and I suggest calming the child at that time and try talking to them a little later, but don't drop the subject they could be being abused or groomed by someone or just know someone who is. Keep talking to your child and let them know you care and they are safe and loved.

My only prayer is that through this book maybe a child will be saved the horrors of sexual abuse, and then I will feel that what I went through was worth it.

I believe the first half of this book can be read to toddlers up to five or six year olds.

And the rest can be read by children alone or with their parents at any age.

My experience in this area comes mostly from my own life experiences with sexual abuse. I've read everything I could find about the healing process, and have been a nurse for 25 years. But in all my research for my own help I never found anything to help prevent this from happening in the first place or to teach children to protect themselves. I was told not to tell after my first incident and didn't know any difference.

So I feel our children need to know it's alright to tell even when told not to.

Thank You and God Bless You,

Teresa Connor

I would like to dedicate this book to my two daughters, Melinda, &

Michaela who encouraged me to finish this book and get it published. Also

to my two granddaughters who are my inspiration to realize that children

need to be educated in this subject to be able to better protect themselves.

GOOD

TOUCH

BAD

TOUCH

Teresa Connor

There are lots of good touches. Hugs and kisses from your parents, family and friends. They make you feel good and let you know that you are special and loved.

1

High fives or a pat on the back when you do a good job, such as scoring a point in

a game or helping out a friend, are also good touches.

Or when you get a good grade on your test or report card. These are all normal

touches that make you feel good about yourself and it lets you know your family

cares.

There are lots of ways those around you make you feel good about yourself, like

telling you that they like the way your hair is styled, or the clothes you are

wearing. Those things make us feel good inside.

There are also touches that just don't feel right, or make you feel uncomfortable.

Sometimes these can be just looks or a funny feeling you get when you are around

someone. It may feel like butterflies in your stomach. This is your body's way of

telling you it is not safe. These are bad touches.

You have private areas of your body that shouldn't be touched by others. Your

private areas are your body parts that are covered by your underwear.

Your private areas were created by God to make you a boy or a girl. These private parts help you to have a family when you grow up and get married.

Your private parts should not be looked at or touched by anyone unless there is

another adult in the room to keep you safe. Usually a Doctor or a Nurse will

examine your private areas during your check up, but even then another adult

should be with you.

Your private parts are areas that God created to make you who you are, and are not

to be abused, or touched in a bad way by others. Try not to be left alone with

someone who makes you feel uncomfortable, or unsafe.

If someone, even a family member, tries to touch you on your private areas, or just

talks to you in a way that scares you, yell for help, or run away if you can.

If someone has touched you in any way that has made you feel afraid, confused, or uncomfortable, tell someone you trust. Tell your Mother, Father, Grandmother, Teacher or a good friend. Most of the time the person who touches you, or tries to touch you, in a bad way will tell you not to tell. They may even tell you that no one will believe you. When they say those things the are just trying to scare you into keeping their secret.

If this has happened to you, you may have confusing thoughts or feelings while

you were being touched or after it happened. These feelings may frighten you and

you may not be sure what these feelings are and if they are good or bad.

If they don't believe you, keep telling until you find someone who believes you.

Sometimes it is hard for families to think someone they know would do that to a

child. That's why some people don't believe you at first, but keep telling until

someone does, they will find you help and the safety you need.

Always remember if this has happened to you, or if it ever does happen to you. It is not your fault! You did nothing wrong. They did. They violated your trust. You are not bad. God made you and you are special. God Loves You just the way you are. You are never alone because He is with you and will help you through this difficult time.

18

SIGNS OF ABUSE TO LOOK FOR:

1. Withdrawing from family or friends.

2. Change in behavior. (Quiet or acting out)

3. Loss of self esteem.

4. Change in grades or school activities

5. Change in the way they dress, such as more covered up.

6.Acting different around a close family member or friend.

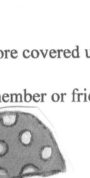

Of course these are basic signs and symptoms that something isn't normal for your

child. It could mean many things from drugs to simply a break-up. But its always

best when you see changes to talk to your child about it You never know they just

may listen and open up to you.

CPSIA information can be obtained at www.ICGtesting.com
Printed in the USA
LVIW01n1426031215
465219LV00017B/96